DREAM CATCHER

a guided journal to uncover your dream and bring it to life

Find more from Kelly Welk at:

@kellywelk
@ciderpresslaneshop

www.ciderpresslane.com
www.dreamcatchercommunity.com

and her first book,
Dinner Changes Everything

DREAM CATCHER

a guided journal to uncover your dream and bring it to life

Kelly Welk

self published by
blurb

Copyright 2018 by Kelly Welk
Edited by Mica DenBleyker
Cover design by Kirsten Judkins

dedicated to our kiddos, that they would be brave enough to follow their hearts

CONTENTS

1::	Dreamers	1
2::	Hello You	9
3::	Space to Listen	19
4::	Cleaning House	27
5::	Start Here	33
6::	Crystal Clear	41
7::	Outsmart It	51
8::	Focus	59
9::	Refining	79
10::	Hop to It	87
11::	Momentum	95
12::	Give	111

DREAMERS

It all began when Aaron and I were newly married. This was my first real chance to have time to cook. I had spent time in the kitchen when I was a kid so I knew the basics, but I'd never been in charge of my own kitchen.

College had been filled with cheese and crackers, quesadillas and cafeteria food. Now, here we were, two kids creating a home and life together and I dove head first into making real food. I loved it.

Every Sunday night we filled our little one bedroom apartment with as many friends as possible. I'd find new recipes and cook up all sorts of things we'd never had before. We would squeeze people around our hand-me-down table and simply enjoy dinner together.

Those Sunday evenings started my dream. The problem was I didn't see it. I knew I loved making food. I knew I loved creating a place for people to connect. I just didn't see how that could be anything more than dinner.

This act of cooking and creating community held no value in my mind or heart beyond exactly what it was: a fun way to hang out with friends. *Come on, let's not be silly, cooking dinner and filling a table with people can't change anyone's life* — at least that's what I thought then.

Fast forward through the last 17 years of our life together—through different jobs, moves, and having kids—and over and over again I see how my love for cooking and filling our table has filled our lives with community and connection. This has been my most powerful tool to bring people together, to inspire, to encourage, support and love on our people.

Then a little shift happened. My heart was asking bigger questions. *What am I really supposed to do with this life of mine? How can I use what I have to help people? How can I use all of our stuff for more than just our own consumption?* It was in these questions that the dream began to surface.

The dream started right where I was most comfortable. It started right where I knew what to do. It started so simple and quiet that I would never have called it the beginning of a dream. Aaron and I invited friends over to eat, but there was a catch. In order to come, everyone would need to bring a donation for an organization we had chosen that fought human trafficking. It seemed like just another dinner. But *this* dinner was different. It gave me the smallest glimpse that this thing that came so naturally to me just might be the most powerful part of my life; it was the beginning of the realization that dinner really could change everything.

Our first dinner didn't look like the beginning of a dream. It looked like friends eating together on a deck. When that evening came to a close, and I realized that this thing that I loved to do could actually be used to help people, a shift began. In the smallest corner of my heart the dream started to grow.

But how do you find 'the dream'? How do you pay attention to what you do best and allow it to grow? Is it important to dream? What if dreaming is only for flighty, irresponsible youth? What if you barely have time to take care of real life, how can you make space to dream and then actually carry it out?

Let's talk about a new kind of dreamer. Let's talk about a new way of living.

This is not about dropping all responsibilities, quitting jobs that provide livelihoods or feeling that unless you sell everything and move to The Bahamas you aren't being true to you. This new way of living looks a lot like normal life, but with the intention to create space to dream and then to take the steps to bring that dream to reality. Whether it be to start a family, launch a business, repaint a bedroom or plant a garden, it's in your *I'd love to some day* or *what if* thoughts that your dreams are rooted.

Every ounce of forward movement in our lives, in our cultures and communities has occurred because someone asked, *What if?* Someone was brave enough to think of something different and new and then have the patience and planning and hard work to see it through. Someone had the freedom to see life from a new perspective. It was the belief in the possibilities that drove them to pursue their dream.

There is something about hoping for the future that motivates our hearts toward it. This hope roots us to our dreams. But most people would never say they are dreamers. Why? Is it because their ideas aren't grand enough, different enough, big enough? Is there a regulation on dream size?

A dream is a cherished aspiration, ambition or ideal.

That means anything that is cherished by *you* that is yet to happen is your dream.

Did you hear that? *Anything*! There are no restrictions on what constitutes a dream. There is also no difference in value. Whether you are dreaming of a cure for cancer or a night around your table with friends, the value remains the same.

    Your dream connects you to who you are and where you want to be - and *that* value is immeasurable. When we silence ourselves, we are saying our hopes aren't valuable. We are inadvertently saying who we are is not important.

    My dreaming started around a table. It turns out that the table is one of my favorite places to be. Sitting with friends and family, enjoying a meal and slowing time down. It seems too simple, but creating this community around our table is where I've found my deepest connection to myself. And that is how all dreams start—with us desiring to do what we love and then finding our deepest contentment in the midst.

    After our first dinner, I started to ask more questions. What would it take to allow our table to help even more women and children caught in human trafficking? Could we host more of these dinners? Could we open them up to more people? Could this table, the dishes in our cellar and food in our cupboards really give freedom? Out of these questions the freedom dinners were born.

    Since that first dinner I've been on a journey and have discovered that I am a dreamer to the core. I'd never seen it in myself because I had never allowed myself to truly dive into the things I loved. I pushed them aside believing they weren't substantial enough. I discounted the things in my life that were just waiting for me to dream over them. I saw being a good hostess as a silly thing to be good at. I wanted to be a world changer with my hands in the salt mines of life. I wanted to do work that was important, I just didn't see how that could happen when I was in the kitchen cooking dinner! Plus, because filling our table with food and friends was easy for me, I didn't think it held any value to others.

    What I've found is that bringing dreams to life sets us on

a deeper course to finding out who we were created to be. When we allow ourselves to go after the things we're thinking or dreaming about, it frees us up to dive even deeper into what we love. Every action step we take toward something we would like to do gives us permission and space to do it again.

Studies show that the regrets people hold onto most are those connected to *NOT* acting upon their ideas and dreams. Sure, we all have regrets about doing something foolish or silly, but the ones that hang on through a lifetime are over the actions we did not take. Our hearts hold strongly to our hopes and dreams, but sometimes we just can't sort out what they are.

There are times in our life where we need a friend to hold a mirror up and say LOOK! Look at what you're good at. Look at how incredible it is when you do _____.

It's hard to see ourselves because what comes naturally to us does not feel like an accomplishment. It does not feel extraordinary. What comes easily turns into our own blind spot. It doesn't even occur to us that these things that come as easily as breathing could ever help someone else. Friends, if you can't see what you're good at, how will you ever know what to dream over so you can become great at it?!

Then there are the What If's. What if the thing I'm dreaming about is so different from what I do now? What if I don't know how to actually make it happen? What if I am a complete novice but I'm dreaming about being an expert? We'll get to that. All of us are starting at the same place, right where we are.

My dad is a dreamer and in every new adventure with him I learned a bit more about what it means to listen to your heart and let it shape your vision for where you're headed.

When I was eight years old, our family set out on one of

the most unique adventures. My dad set goals for himself and his business and when he reached those goals, we sold everything, packed up the house, and left Alaska to move to a small marina in Washington to live on a 42" Krogan, a small classic looking yacht.

For almost three years that boat was home. The best part about it was that this home did not seem strange to me in the least. Isn't it normal to have the docks and schools of jellyfish as your front yard?

My brother, who was five at the time, lived in a life jacket. We grew up on the decks of that boat, polished brass as one of our chores, and learned to paddle a dinghy and steer the boat just like some kids learn to drive tractors or push lawn mowers. We spent the summers going around the San Juan Islands and also traveled the intracoastal waterway from Texas to Virginia. We lived out Dad's dream as if that were the most normal thing ever, because it was. He showed us first hand what it looked like to listen to your heart, make plans and then take action to bring a dream to life.

My dad continues to teach his kids that being a dreamer does not mean that you have your head stuck in the clouds. Being a dreamer is a gift. Dreamers can see the potential in someone or something and then take the steps to make it happen. But even with all of this great hands-on training from my dad, it took me stumbling into my own dream for me to discover it!

It's a dangerous business uncovering your dreams. It is not for the faint of heart. To be a dreamer is to see your own potential, to be your biggest fan, your loudest advocate and your most loyal supporter.

Dreamers believe deeply in who they are and how they can impact their world. There is no limit to how big your heart can dream, but first let's create space for your heart to speak and for you to listen.

This journal is just that: space for you to see your potential and then take the steps to bring it to life. There won't be one *right* way or a perfect idea, one correct answer or a specific formula to follow. This is about YOU uncovering the life you dream of.

DREAM CATCHER

HELLO YOU

If you could blink and have it in your hand—the finished product, the ambition, the idea, the goal, the life—what would it be? It's okay if it is unclear. It's okay if you change your mind. It's okay if it sounds too big or too small or too crazy! There is no *right* answer. So be wild and write down what you would do if nothing was holding you back.

But what if you stare at this space and draw a complete blank? No words flow from your pen. What if you look around and you just aren't sure which parts of your life are actually a reflection of your truest self? What if your heart has been on pause for so long that you really aren't sure what you like? What if the reality of life has drowned out it's voice?

It's time, my friend, to make space for your heart to speak. Do you know its voice? I know you've heard it before; it was your constant companion as a kid. It said, *When I grow up I'm going to* _____. There was nothing that could stop you. You could be and do anything.

_____

DREAM CATCHER

If I could do anything, I would .....

Have you heard that voice lately? The one that says, *I like hiking; I'm gonna clear Saturday morning to go hike with the family. I like cooking; I wonder if our friends could come for dinner on Friday. I love gardening; I'm going to clean out that garden bed and plant flowers this weekend.*

You know that shy friend of yours, the one who is super talkative once you get to know them? They are just like your heart. It is shy. It is waiting for you to take time to recognize its voice. Once you do, it will become your constant companion. It will say, *I love doing this simply because*, and you'll lean in to listen because you've learned to trust it.

Leaning in and listening to your heart can feel awkward. We aren't used to slowing down long enough to hear it, but it is a practice that is necessary for our long term endurance. It is a practice that is necessary for us to know ourselves. Even though the listening might feel awkward, taking a chance to act on what our heart is speaking, feeling, dreaming, or directing may feel downright crazy.

When I met my friend Carolyn she had just started planting her first flower field. One day, earlier that year, she was reading a magazine in her office cubicle about two women who had become farmer florists and something sparked in her heart. She brought that magazine home to show her husband, Pip. When she said, *I want to do this*, God bless Pip! His response was what every heart needs to hear, *Go for it! What's the worst that could happen? We'll have a garden full of beautiful flowers?*

That spring Carolyn tilled up a couple of patches of their property and planted the beginning of her flower farm. Now, four years later, Carolyn is a full time flower farmer working her dream and listening to her heart as the business and flower fields expand and grow. It all started right there in the stirring of her heart.

Carolyn had never run a flower farming business. She'd never even worked for one. She just knew that she loved flowers and liked working in the dirt. And on that winter day in her gray office cubicle she was able to lean in just enough to hear her heart say, *I like this!*

What if your heart says, *I love music!* but you've never picked up an instrument? What if your heart says, *I love to paint,* but you see no value in painting? What if your heart says, *I would love to go back to school!* but you don't believe it's possible?

This is a mining process, where you sift through all of the excess in order to find buried treasure. And you can start digging right here in your everyday life. There are diamonds buried under the busyness that define you—these are the treasures you are searching for.

Pour yourself a steaming cup of coffee or tea or your favorite bubbly drink and break out your calendar so you can look at everything—E V E R Y T H I N G —you currently do.

Write it all down—school, work, cleaning, taking care of friends, family or kids, what you do in the mornings, evenings, weekends, vacations—jot it all down. You need to see it on these pages. You need to see the life you are living.

This is not a time to write, *Workout twice a day, seven days a week*, if that is not what you really do. This is not an I-wish-my-weeks-looked-like-this kind of list. This is a list of what you already do now. It's important for you to see *the now* because *now* is exactly where you must begin.

———————————————————

HELLO YOU

Mornings :

Evenings :

Family :

DREAM CATCHER

Friends :

Work :

Free Time :

Now scan over this list of things that fill your days and underline everything—EVERYTHING—that stands out that you LOVE (or even kind of like) to do. Highlight the areas where you are already creating. Color the areas where you are meeting your heart.

(Hint hint—if you're stumped you might need to ask a friend to help you see where these places are. Are you already painting, writing, refurbishing furniture, taking photos for friends, growing flowers and gardens, volunteering, loving on kids, creating art, fashioning jewelry, hosting dinners, sewing, building, running, cooking, baking, counseling, tutoring?)

Now you're going to take each one of the underlined or highlighted things and write out all the reasons why you like them. Some of these might feel like deep answers, others are going to feel a bit frivolous, but all of them matter. Do not discount something on this list because it doesn't *feel* very important. Most likely the ones you easily discount are actually where your super powers are hidden.

DREAM CATCHER

What are you already doing that you love & why?
(Fill these pages with every single idea!)

I am sure you are thinking, *Why are we only looking at what we're already doing? Aren't we supposed to be thinking about some big dream? The big dream surely is not connected to what I already do!*

Those were the exact thoughts that would go through my head when I was searching for that deeper connection between my life and finding meaning. I grew up learning about a God that created us on purpose and for a purpose. I believed it, I knew it to be true, but I just could not figure out what mine was. When people would ask, *What are you passionate about? What's your purpose in life?* I would feel like a deer caught in the headlights.

Sure, I loved Jesus, and I was going to keep loving on my husband and kids. Of course I had all of the must-do daily bits of life. But I thought that my big connection to a life of meaning was going to come from a new idea outside of my normal day-to-day. That thought right there was my biggest trap.

We are blinded from seeing our purpose when we think that our meaning in life is *not* connected to our everyday.

If our deepest purpose is always out on the horizon, how will we ever feel like our simple everyday acts are meaningful? We look at our daily grind of the same old things and can't see the power that is right there in day-to-day rituals. We miss the deep meaning that is waiting to be discovered in everyday living and this discovery requires space to see it. It is time for you to see yours.

DREAM CATCHER

SPACE TO LISTEN

We have three kids and all of them have the most important thing to say all at the same time. It does not bother them in the least that their voice is being drowned out by other voices.

If the phone rings it is their cue to start talking to me immediately. It's funny, but maddening. The interesting thing is that they all have the desire to be heard, but they're still learning the art of listening.

In a world moving at the speed of light, with thousands of messages bombarding us on a daily basis I'm going to venture to say we are all still learning the art of listening. It isn't just about listening though, this is about creating space to hear. This, my friend, is the most important skill to learn.

The reality is, in order to move forward on your dream you must learn how to listen to your own heart. But what does it look like to create space for this new kind of listening, for time to think, pray or reflect? For some it will look like journaling, for others, walking, yoga, drawing, or maybe being still - eyes closed. But, for all, this space will contain a quietness.

The quiet feels deafening at first but I challenge you to embrace it. It takes practice to learn how to quiet our minds so we can hear our hearts. Begin by giving yourself five minutes of silence to simply sit in stillness and concentrate on the sound of your own breathing. You were created to rest and pause in order for your heart to speak.

Okay, so you are sitting in the quiet, listening to your breath. Is your mind wandering? Are you thinking, *Now what am I supposed to do*? It's natural for our minds to wander. It's natural to start thinking about all of the tasks and to-do lists that need to be accomplished. Take this time of quiet to direct your own thoughts.

Let's go back to that list you wrote down of what you loved in your life and why (page 31). Let's think on those things. You can start by asking yourself these questions.

Do you see anything in common between the things you like to do?

Do you remember other times in your life that you did similar things?

How do you feel when you have time to do these things?

DREAM CATCHER

Are there ways that you would like to spend more time in these areas?

You will naturally be drawn to the things you enjoy. You will naturally try to fit those into your life. Maybe you aren't DOING them to your full potential yet but you are reading about them, thinking about them, or creating in a small way now. This is an important piece to realize because not every season looks the same, yet there will be commonalities between them.

When Aaron and I were first married I was just learning how to cook. I would buy new ingredients and test out meals we had never even heard of before, not just because I loved cooking but because I loved creating community around our table.

Then we had our first baby. I kept cooking because quite simply it made me happy beyond the required *I must make food because we need to eat* function of it. When our second and third kids came along, most afternoons you would find us all lined up along the kitchen counter mixing up banana bread or scones, trying out a new risotto recipe or rolling out pizza dough.

We hosted dinners and brought meals to other families. We baked cakes for neighborhood block parties and cooked for holiday gatherings. Cooking kept me connected to me, but, more so, it was a way I connected with others. It was life giving during a time when I was giving most of myself to what my kids needed.

Now our kids are in school and the act of cooking to create community continues to be what defines our life together. Our traditions stem from it, our schedules reflect its importance, my entire business is now built around my initial desire to create community around good food. Cooking is deeply intertwined with so many areas of my life and over many different seasons.

You have the same areas in your life. There will be a common thread through different seasons and stages. It is important that you see yours. *Not* what you think it should look like but what it truly is. This reflection takes stillness and space to think so you can step back and see your life from a different perspective. Until you create time to slow down, you will not be able to see where you are.

This practice of becoming still to think and pray and meditate is not a one-time gig. This is a continual, weekly (sometimes daily) practice that will help you stay focused and centered on who you were created to be. It is vital for your dream to come to life.

What time(s) this week are you blocking out to think, reflect, pray?

SPACE TO LISTEN

What ideas and thoughts continue to come to the surface during these times?

Are there certain feelings that you cannot shake?

DREAM CATCHER

Are there any ideas that continue to stir in your heart?

_____

    Now let's get ready to take action on what your heart has been saying! Let's make space for you to do more of what your heart has been talking about.

CLEANING HOUSE

Spending time in the stillness to listen to your heart is refreshing. But if you're looking at your journal and thinking how do I transfer that peace and clarity to my life? How do I make time to actually do the things I'm interested in?

Deep breaths here—this is not about cramming more stuff into an already overflowing calendar. This is about evaluating your commitments so you can create time for the activities that are tethered to your heart.

I love the Proverb that says, *As water reflects the face, so one's life reflects the heart.* When our hearts are feeling overwhelmed it reflects in a chaotic and frantic life. Just as when our hearts feel at peace it reflects in our living with intention and purpose.

Life is full of *must-dos* like work and cleaning, taking care of kids and loved ones, laundry, groceries, studying. We're not talking about shirking responsibilities or saying yes to everything. This is about finding the margin. Yes, I know it's hard! But, it is in the margins that you will have space to create what your heart is speaking to you about.

Do you have any margin in your life? Is every day packed from sun up till sun down? Are you looking at your schedule thinking I barely have time to breathe let alone do something just for the sake of creating.

Then it's time to do the hard work of saying no to the extras that are taking away from you chasing your dream. In order for you to say yes to doing more of what brings you life, you have to say no to those activities that are taking up the extra space.

It's hard to see what to cut out so consider beginning by saying no to new things. Say no to extra commitments so you can start saying yes to creating space for you. It's going to feel a bit foreign at first but we must remember that we cannot do what we have always done and expect to get to a new destination.

Confession on my part, there were several years of my life where I was addicted to watching Biggest Loser. The transformation the people would make was astounding. These women who could barely walk a mile were running marathons by the end, you could not even recognize them!

How did they do it? It wasn't just because they started eating different, or working out, it was because they reworked their entire lives. The individuals that could barely get off the couch in the beginning started new habits of getting up to run before work. They rearranged there schedules, made new priorities, stopped the daily doughnut shop runs and started spending that time at the gym. It wasn't just that they recovered their health, their new habits and schedules created new lives.

This is the same thing we need to do. Our calendars can easily pack on the pounds and feel a bit glutinous. It's time to shed the excess busyness. Not sure where to begin? It might be time for another date with you. Let's go back to creating space to think. Maybe it's an evening to yourself or a quiet morning to really look at your calendar.

Think of it like this, if someone plopped you down on a tilt-a-whirl, turned the ride on full speed and then asked you to explain the landscape around you, how do you think you'd do? This is exactly what busyness does to our lives. It's all whizzing by too fast to really pinpoint any one thing. Your tilt-a-whirl is going too fast to really see what commitments you can say no to.

Busyness causes unintentional blindness.

When life is too full, too rushed, or too packed there is just too much of everything. You cannot see if you are headed in any direction other than running in circles. It's time to create space for reflection where you can step off of the ride to see the landscape-where you hit pause so you can hear your heart speak.

This isn't about doing nothing all the time, it's about intentional pauses so you can look up, catch your breath and make sure you're still heading towards your dream. These pauses help you see what direction you need to move in. They help you see what activities are necessary.

Take some time right now to schedule that date with yourself this week, next month, next quarter and next year. These dates will help you stay on track. These questions apply over and over again regardless of how many steps we've taken towards our dream.

DREAM CATCHER

What activities/commitments are feeding your dream?

CLEANING HOUSE

Are there activities/commitments that are taking away from it, or maybe they are taking up extra time needlessly?

If so, can you say no to them in the future?

As you make space for your heart you are giving it permission to speak. Lean in when you have these moments to pause. Refuse to let busyness drown out your heart. The space you are creating is where your dream is beginning to take shape.

START HERE

You're doing it. Making space in your life. Creating a clear picture of what you want to be about. So now what, how do you actually start?

Do you have a mental Pinterest board full of ideas of where you want to be or what you want to create? A mental image of what you're hoping for? I bet it's shiny, bright and picture perfect. I'm guessing you're staring at it and wondering how do you get from where you are today to *this*? I bet you are feeling a bit like climbing back into that safe and comfortable old schedule.

Let's take that pinterest perfect image and poke a few holes in it so you can see where to begin.

Right here.
Stop reading for a second, look up.
Look around you.
This is where you are going to start.
Right here in your everyday life.

Remember those things you underlined or highlighted that you loved about your life? That's where you're starting. You don't need brand new tools, shoes, decor, tables, chairs, you name it. You already have what you need. How have you been doing what you loved currently? Start with that.

When I met my friend Anya I had no idea she loved writing. Our daughters were friends from school and through hanging out at the park and going trick or treating for Halloween we became friends. Then one day she said she was going to publish her first novel. Oh my word, did I celebrate with her! What an incredible accomplishment. That's when she started sharing more about how writing had kept her grounded when her kids were little. She would steal moments here and there to create characters and other realities through her words. She wrote during those years of raising babies into toddlers not because anyone else was reading it, but because it gave her life. It was the act of *doing* not just dreaming that brought purpose to the writing.

During those years she did what she could to write. She didn't push it aside because it couldn't be a job at that point. She didn't avoid creating because no one else was seeing it. She didn't forget about it because she couldn't do it properly. She just wrote for the sake of writing. She wrote because it brought joy. Every hour she spent then was preparing her for what she does now. Now writing is her full time job. She spends her days crafting and creating new stories and worlds and characters. Now she has an office and business built around this thing that for years was just between her and her computer screen. She started right where she was, with what she had, doing what she could in that season.

When we hosted our first Freedom Dinner, I pulled out all of our random dishes, mismatched tablecloths, goblets and silverware and set two tables that were different shapes and sizes. I didn't have the farm tables and lights, chairs and goblets, or the connections in the community like I do now. What I did have was years of cooking. Years of feeding friends and filling our table that gave me the confidence to take the first step. That first dinner was my starting line.

START HERE

You have the same starting line right where you are. Want to start styling photos? Start with what you have. Practice with different pieces and lighting, backgrounds and presets. Want to start a new workout routine? Start with what you have: the comfy sweats, your seemingly old tennis shoes, a walk around the block.

Sinking hundreds of dollars into the latest trends, fads or even classes is not necessarily the best first step. First, spend time doing this thing that you think you like. Spend time figuring out if you want to do it more. Then, as it grows and you learn more about yourself and the bits that you love, *then* start investing in it.

There are so many ways that your dream is already taking shape as you create space to do more of what you love. Sometimes we just have to point it out to ourselves so we can see where to begin.

It's easy for our minds to try to complicate this, we think:

In order to start, I need to be ready.
In order to start, I need to have the best gear.
In order to start, I need to have everything figured out.

Our minds can easily stop us. The reality is in order to start you simply need the desire to take the first step. That's it. You don't have to understand or map out the entire course. You don't even have to completely know where you're headed. You just need to be willing to move. Let's keep it simple right now and take time to inventory what's around you.

What do I enjoy doing, and what do I already have to do this

(cameras, tools, computer)?

This right here, these things that you are great at, this is where your dream starts. Right here where it almost feels normal. Right here, one step out of your comfort zone, using what you have with new intentions.

Here's the second part to this: now that you see what you are doing and what you have, fill the extra space you are creating on your calendar with these things.

It might not be clear yet in your own mind how you want to see this dream grow. How you can use it to bring people together or how it will help others. That's okay! It's in the doing that you'll sort out more of how you want to spend your time. The question of how can it grow is best answered when you're in the midst of creating.

Creativity is a muscle; the more you use it, the stronger it gets. Creating more inspires more. Right now the most important thing is to simply begin. Make stuff that you'll never show another soul. Paint pictures no one will ever see. Bake cakes that are lopsided and burned. Run races even though you get last place. Play music no one will ever hear. Do it because your muscles need to get warmed up.

———————————————

DREAM CATCHER

What are you going to start 'creating' this week?

START HERE

What days/times are you setting aside to create?

DREAM CATCHER

What will you need?

These first steps are the hardest. You're unsure of yourself and a bit shaky. It's okay! You're creative muscles will get stronger. These first steps are some of the most important because each one is shouting to the rooftops (at least in your own mind and heart) that YOU believe in yourself, and that, my friend, is the most important place to be.

CRYSTAL CLEAR

Are you ready for them? The questions, the ideas, the thoughts? They are going to come from every corner of your life. From people who genuinely want to help and others who might not. But guess what? ALL of the questions are good. Why aren't you around to do X, Y and Z? Why aren't you available to help with this volunteer opportunity? Why aren't you responding to text messages fast enough, to emails immediately, to phone calls? Why aren't you doing what you used to do? Why aren't you taking more customers? Why aren't you expanding your business?

Welcome all of the questioning, the should-dos and ideas. Sure they're maddening—they're going to make you feel like you're letting people down. They will make you question if you're doing the right thing. They will bring up fear of what others will think, if you're doing enough or being enough. And all of those fears and thoughts and questions are good. They are crucial to you sorting out who you are, how you want your life to be structured, how you want to schedule your days, how you envision your future—what you're about and what you value. But here's the trick. The questioning does not dictate what you do, your answers to the questions define the exact direction you want to go. I know it feels harsh, but this is where *YOUR HEART* gets to be the loudest voice.

It's extremely hard to stay true to yourself in the midst of other people's ideas. What makes sense to one person might not be what is best for you. When I was a kid and our family moved out of Alaska to become the 'boat family', I remember people questioning my parents. People, who did not know them well, thought they were out of their minds to sell everything and leave a successful business. With well intentioned words, they advised them against it. But my parents knew that what made sense to others was not what dictated the decisions they made. The path that other people chose was not theirs. My parents had been adventuring together for so long that what felt crazy to some, felt normal to them. I can only imagine how suffocating it would have felt had they chosen to do what everyone else thought was right.

The same is true for my friends whose deepest desire is to create a homestead, to grow their own vegetables, raise their own chickens and dig deep deep roots in their communities. To force them off the land and onto a boat would have pushed them into a life their heart would not have chosen.

Embracing a crystal clear vision for your dream gives you freedom to design it exactly how your heart sees it. This clarity keeps you true to what you know is right for you. So embrace all of the questioning and the well intentioned advice. Hear it and then allow it to help you shape your direction.

The questions act a bit like spring cleaning, where you go through every nook and cranny of your dream—every commitment, job, task, and responsibility connected to it—and refine it all down. You can use the answers to those questions to create a mission statement for your life. This statement will be like a compass for you as you determine what new opportunities you will go after and which ones simply don't line up.

Your mission statement will help determine your direction. It helps you stay focused on what you are saying is most important to you. When you are invited to join a new team or take on a new project, create a new piece of art, or simply decide if you are free for a weekend, you'll have your guide for what you are saying yes to. For a season it might feel like you are saying no to everything. That's okay. It takes time to shift your personal focus and it isn't until your family, friends and community see that your focus has shifted that they will start inviting you to be involved in ways that are aligned to your new way of living.

Let's say you currently spend a lot of time at the coffee shop but you want to spend more time at the gym. The first couple weeks of you shifting your focus there will be a lot of friends who are still sending invites to the coffee shop. You will feel like you're saying no all the time. Then everyone sees you spending more time at the gym. Not just for a week or two but for weeks and months. Now you're getting invites to meet up for a specific yoga class, or opportunities to join groups at the gym. The invitation shift is happening.

Now it's time for the fun part. It's time to start putting into words what it is you *do* want your life and dream to be about. I encourage you to be as SPECIFIC as you can. Your personal mission statement is not set in stone, it will shift and change as your dream does. There are no correct answers so don't stress over this. In fact, you already have the beginning of your definition in the previous chapters!

Look back on the areas of your current schedule that you underlined or highlighted, those things that you love. All of those activities, relationships, and projects are showing you what you want your life to be about!

Now is your chance to write down your own mission statement. This will be your guide as you continue to create intentional space to bring your dream to life. Here are a few of my favorite reminders as you declare what you are about!

We do not do things because:
- Someone else does them
- Someone else wants us to do them
- Someone else thinks we should do them
- Or even because we *can* do them!

**We shape our lives around what
WE choose to be about.**

You'll notice there isn't very much space to fill out. I'm serious about keeping it simple. Defining what our life is about declares to ourself how we will use our time to go after the things we care about, and since time is limited we must keep our focus limited to only those things that are most important.

Living a life of intention takes a whole lot of intention! Meditate on these following questions. Pray and ask God for clarity of mind. Pause and listen. Then jot down the simple phrases that come to mind.

CRYSTAL CLEAR

What do you want your life to be about?

Now that you have written down your own mission statements, here's a BIG QUESTION for your reflection time. Are there more things you need to cut out of your schedule that do not align with this statement?

THIS TAKES COURAGE.

The things you are writing down here may not be bad, they might actually be good! The goal is not to do lots of good things, the goal is to do the few things that are deeply rooted to what you want your life to be about.

Is there anything else you need to cut out of your schedule?

Refining what you say yes to takes time. Staying true to a clear vision for where you are headed is a process. The more you pursue the things you love the clearer your vision will be for where you are going.

It's like when you were a kid and someone asked, what kind of dessert do you like? EVERYTHING. I like all dessert. I'll eat anything with sugar! The big concept is that you know you like sugar. As you get older and you try all sorts of different desserts you realize there are some that are definitely your favorite. Now, as an adult, if someone were to ask you what kind of dessert you like, you probably have just a few things that come to mind. Your taste is much more refined. You know exactly what you would choose.

How we design our days and go after our dreams is the same way. We start pretty broad, with big statements. *I want to create community. I want to create art. I want to teach people to be healthy.* Then we start doing more things that are true to those statements and our broad statements become narrower until our vision truly is laser focused.

One of the biggest challenges as you go from the broad statement to the laser focus is that the more people see you succeeding in the areas you love, the more invitations you will have for opportunities! Bingo, this is what you want, right? Keep your mission statement in mind. It's exciting to be recognized for the work you are doing. It's flattering when you get invited to use your craft to be involved with others, but not every invitation is worthy of a yes. Following your heart does not create an immunity to needless activity. If anything, it has a tendency to create more opportunity for it. The excitement you feel when you get to teach or garden, farm or run marathons, makes it even harder to say no when you are invited to do those exact things! The concept of busyness remains the same: if you are too busy doing too much, you will miss the true opportunities to follow your own dream.

I'll hold your hand through this because I know how hard it is. What do you do when someone is looking you straight in the eye and saying, *I love having you on this team! Will you help out again? We need you in this program. I can't do it without you!*

Gulp! I've been there—staring at people thinking, *I cannot say yes. This is their vision, their dream, their project, their to-do list, not mine.* But what do you say?! How do you say no without offending?

Let's try to make it a bit easier. This isn't about saying *NO* flat out. I know you care about these people. Fill in your own words so that when you are bombarded and pressured to say yes, you'll ready with a kind *no*.

'I am honored that you would think of me, unfortunately I do not have any more space in my calendar.'

'I love what you are doing, it's incredible and I'm cheering you on. I'd love to send people your way if I can, but unfortunately I'm not free.'

(*Remember! It is NOT your responsibility to explain why you do not have space; your schedule is your own).

IF IF IF it is something that MIGHT fit with your personal mission statement: 'Thank you for thinking of me. Can I get back to you next week? I need to make sure it will work for our schedule.'

Saying yes immediately is rarely the right answer. Even if you think, *this is everything I want to do!*, let yourself think on it. Bounce the idea off at least one person you respect, a person who knows you, your heart and what you want your life to be about. They will help you make sure you're staying true to your tunnel vision.

―――――――――――――

Who do you trust to bounce ideas off of?

What do they think?

DREAM CATCHER

What will need to change in order for you to have space and time for this new opportunity?

It's hard to be intentional with our time. But it is easier when you have given yourself a crystal clear vision to stay focused on.

OUTSMART IT

We like to think that outside circumstances are our biggest hurdles: finances, time, schedules, people—you name it. Rarely do we realize that *we* create our biggest obstacles. I'm going to venture to say that as you filled these pages with ideas and hopes another voice started to speak louder than your own. Let's talk about that voice because plain and simple, that voice is fear and it is good at welcoming itself into every corner of your mind.

Fear is sneaky. It masks itself in every costume it can find. It creeps into your quiet thoughts nicely disguised as your own and says that you don't have what it takes. But rarely is it kind enough to be that straightforward. Instead it whispers in your ear as you scan social media, it mocks your ability after an important conversation, it highlights your deficiencies while looking at friends or competitors.

Fear shows up in so many disguises that we don't recognize it. It is cunning and incredibly patient. It knows our weaknesses and will wave them on display, showing us over and over again until discouragement wears us down and our own voice is almost impossible to hear.

You know your heart, you know it's voice. It's the one you heard as you filled these pages with everything you wanted to create space for. That was *you* talking, straight from your heart, about the things you've dreamed could fill your life.

Your voice is your greatest advocate but fear is its strongest competitor and it gains power in silence. Your voice—your speaking-out-loud, talking voice—will be your greatest tool to stop it.

It's time to drag fear out of the shadows. Write down what fear is saying to you. Share what you are feeling with friends and then find the flaws in these fears so you can use them as fuel to move you forward.

Deep breath, friend. You can do this. It takes immense courage to put words and voice behind the thoughts that are running through our minds. You may be thinking, *Am I the only one who feels this way? What will people think of me? What if I don't have what it takes?*

Guess what? You are not alone. I have those same thoughts. Your voice will free you.

What fears are running through your head? 'I'm not talented enough', 'I don't know enough', 'I'm not skilled enough...'

continued ... What fears are running through your head?

Okay, I see those fears. I have a long list of my own. We all do. Remember that family member, or spouse, or friend you chatted with about your mission statement? Make a date with them to sit down or facetime and talk about these fears. You NEED another set of eyes looking at your life, looking at *you* and helping you see clearly.

When can you meet? Make a date; this is an important conversation!

When you meet, share your fears openly and clearly. Then take time to look at each fear together. Talk about if there is any validity to it and what you can do to combat it. For every tag line that fear whispers in your ear, you have two options in response: 1. agree with it and let it stop you or 2. figure out what action will silence it.

FEAR : I'm not talented enough.
ACTION : Educate yourself, take a class, go to a workshop.

FEAR : I don't know where to start.
ACTION : Find a mentor, someone you admire that is a couple steps ahead, and ask for help.

FEAR : I don't know how to do _____.
ACTION : Ask for help or hire someone who is great at this particular skill.

Stepping toward fear, looking it square in the eye and fighting the urge to let it stop you, is hard work.

I wish I could say that you can conquer fear once and for all. But the truth is that as long as you are continuing to move forward, you will always be stepping into new territory which gives fear more opportunities to try and barricade the way.

Here's the good news: it gets easier to beat fear as you set up strategies to overcome it.

1. Write the fears down
2. Talk them out
3. Take action to prove the fear wrong.

Now let's take time to write down those fears again. Now that you've brainstormed with your trusted someone, fill in the action you are going to take to prove the fear wrong. Be specific. Find the class you're going to take and register for it. Do you need to find help with your website? Create a new routine or habit? Give yourself a time frame and write down when you'll be meeting with said experts. The more specific you are, the easier it is to accomplish the action step.

Be KIND to yourself. No need to be Superwoman and try to conquer every fear this week. Be reasonable. Tackle one at a time and let the success in each area move you further from fear and closer to confidence.

FEAR :

ACTION:

FEAR:

ACTION:

FEAR:

ACTION:

FEAR :

ACTION:

FEAR :

ACTION:

FEAR :

ACTION:

FEAR :

ACTION:

FOCUS

Our family loves the Olympics. Watching the athletes become the best in the world is inspiring, but my favorite part is the stories—when they break away from the competition and give us a look into the lives behind those 30 seconds of glory. You get a small glimpse into the focus and devotion it takes to be the best. The reason the stories are inspiring is because every single one of them is telling us that it's possible.

It's possible for Mikaela Shiffrin, a small town girl from Colorado who grew up on the mountain slopes, to take her love of skiing and become the youngest slalom champion in Olympic history.

It's possible for Jessica Diggins and Kikkan Randall to win the United States' first ever cross-country skiing gold medal.

It's possible for the underdog to come out as the best.

But these achievements didn't just happen. The lives leading up to these races were intentional and laser focused. Every bit of their lives revolved around their goal, to become the best athlete in their sport. There are stories just like these in every aspect of our communities where realtors are becoming the best realtor they can be, stories of master gardeners and teachers, musicians and writers. The commonality between all of them is focus. Each of these individuals took one area and dove headlong into it allowing it to capture all of their attention.

There is something really amazing that happens when we zoom in on one thing. When we allow ourselves to devote our attention fully to something, we are able to see the fine details, its nuances and textures, and our appreciation and understanding for it deepens. We too have the capability of being at our best when we devote our time and attention to one area.

The question is how do you keep that laser-like focus when you don't have a team of trainers, nutritionists and sponsors guiding your everyday activities and calendar. What does it look like in real life to keep the focal point of the mission statement you wrote for yourself?

I've found there is a bit of a catch 22 in this: when you start diving deeper into the things you love, people take notice. It's magnetic. They see you living out a life that is fulfilled and of course they want to connect. This is a WIN, right? And that's the catch. Their thoughts, opinions and ideas for you will pop up continually. If you aren't careful, they can steer your heart off course.

Come join us on this committee, we're doing exactly what you're doing!

Come be part of this event, we're doing exactly what you're doing!

Come collaborate with us on this project, we're doing exactly what you're doing!

The question isn't whether or not what they are doing is good, the question is, is this good for YOU? Or, even better, does this activity or investment keep you focused on the dream YOU are shaping?

I'll be honest, sometimes it's not clear! Wouldn't it be great if it was always a black and white situation: if you step out into the rain you will get wet, if you save $50 every month your savings will grow. Opportunity is full of gray unknowns, which makes it hard to pass up! Maybe that open door will lead to where you want to be. Then again, you might walk through it and realize it's not where you were wanting to go.

After we had been hosting the Freedom Dinners for a while, people started asking if I would cater their party, provide lunch for their team meeting or run the catering team for their wedding or office fundraiser. All of these requests made me pause. Was I missing the mark? Should I get my catering license?

The deeper I dove into the questions the clearer it became to me that even though I love creating fresh-from-the-garden menus and filling our table with people, catering was not for me. Sure, I could have done these jobs for the experience of it. I could have done them to help people out or even simply because they would have paid. But none of those reasons had anything to do with following what my heart was nudging me towards.

At the same time, what our business looks like now is drastically different from when it began. All of the events and weddings that I've designed, all of the flowers I've arranged, dinners that I have run, and groups that I've spoken at have all helped shape and cement exactly what I am about: giving freedom by creating community.

My focus now is so much clearer than it was four years ago, but I could not have started this journey knowing what I know now. It's the nature of doing that helps us see clearer.

You will *need* to get your feet wet in all sorts of little ponds in order to find where you feel most at home. The trick is to remember that opportunities are not obligations.

Opportunities are questions that you get to answer. Look at the opportunity held up against your mission statement. Does it fit the dream you are creating? Make the best decision you can based on what you know now, based on what *you* are wanting to focus on.

The catch with opportunities is that they are flattering, and who doesn't love to be flattered!? When you're asked to be on a team, or to take the lead on a project, it's telling you that this person believes in you. They think you're capable and skilled at what you do. It's only natural to want to say yes.

People will rave about their own ideas and how what they are doing is right for you; they'll invite you into their dreams, they'll give you spaces and places to plant yours. It takes time to find the perfect fit. There is no exact formula. What fits as a creative outlet for one person may or may not fit for you. We're all shaped differently. It comes down to being honest with yourself when you pause to listen to what your heart is directing you to do.

Continue the practice of blocking out time to think about your life and what you're creating. This requires that same kind of quiet that you gifted yourself when you started this journal. Continually carve out that quiet so your heart can speak.

———————————————

What day/time this week can you take to be still and quiet?

Guard this time. Do not bail on meeting with yourself. Every 'meeting' you show up to for yourself tells your heart you value its voice! You would never just not show up to a coffee date with a friend, or schedule appointments and then not go. Treat your heart with that same respect; you'll be amazed at how much you can answer about your life and what you want it to be about when your heart feels valued.

These solo coffee dates or calendar meetings are when you get to ask yourself how you're feeling. What's working? What isn't? Is the calendar getting too full again? There is no clear road map when it comes to dreaming. Oh, it would be lovely if you could simply ask Siri to give you directions. 'Siri, take me to exactly where I'm supposed to be!'

The good news is, you have your own internal compass and asking questions helps you find your way. Think of the following questions as guardrails to keep you from veering off course and losing your direction. You might drive like a bumper car for a while, bouncing off of this idea and that opportunity. Give yourself the space to bounce. It's okay to drive like a kid on a carnival ride! The bumps (and maybe a few bruises) will continually help to refocus your heart and this, in turn, will keep you on the road to fulfilling your dream.

DREAM CATCHER

Here are a few questions to ask yourself during your quiet time:

Am I creating the life I was dreaming about?

Does this new opportunity give or take away from the life I want to create?

Does it allow me to be true to myself?

How do I feel when I'm a part of it?

DREAM CATCHER

What part works?

What part doesn't?

FOCUS

What am I giving up?

What am I gaining?

There is an excitement when you dive into what you love. There is an eagerness to engage with as much as possible. When you find your place, it's as if you just can't get enough. Be faithful to continue to meet with yourself because this excitement has the tendency to create a busyness that is deafening. You need to continually hear your heart speaking and guiding.

Busyness can drown out your joy EVEN if it is connected to what you love. Doing more is not better, it's just more. Keeping your focus will also keep the joy.

The trickiest part? You can't measure your own "overwhelm threshold" by what someone else can handle. If it's too much for you, it's too much. But how do you know it's too much? Can you tell when you're getting too close to your threshold?

My failsafe 'too full' meter goes off if I start thinking, *Let's just ditch everything and leave.* Or, *Maybe I'll get sick and won't have to take care of any of this.*

Or when I start feeling a sense of dread when I think about certain commitments or projects.

Or when I no longer have time to make dinner for our family or even think about inviting people over.

Your failsafe meters will sound and feel different from mine, do you know them? Take some time to think about what triggers yours.

_____

FOCUS

What sounds the alarm for your 'too much' meter?

When I think .....

When I feel .....

When I stop having time for .....

Keeping your focus is like cleaning out closets, there will be a constant clearing out of the unnecessary—the random ideas that are good but not in line with your bigger picture, the thoughts and opportunities everyone else will have for you. Ideas are a dime a dozen; there will always be new, shiny ones. But just because a penny is new and shiny does not make it more valuable; what gives it value is when it gains compounded interest.

When you invest more and more time into where your heart is, it's like filling your bank account—the value grows as you stay consistent. If you continually jump on the bright and shiny new ideas, the compounding effect never has time to take root.

Dreams are the same, they cannot take shape if you are always chasing new ones.

So, welcome people's suggestions. There might be something to them that will help you understand your own thoughts better. There might be something to them that will help you reach more people. Then again, they may just be shiny pennies.

During a season of big growth for my business I was getting inundated with event requests. My calendar was filling up with weddings and company parties and all I could think about was how much I wanted to fill my own table with community, how much I wanted to draw people together to pause and enjoy life, how much I wanted to encourage other women to find their own dream, how much I wanted to leverage the power of community to give freedom.

I kept dumping all of my own ideas into my 'dream bank' and picking up more shiny pennies. As I was taking on more of what other people were presenting to me, the business was taking on a shape that was different than what my heart was leaning toward. When it came time to plan the next year for our family and business, I realized the focus of the business had shifted away from the direction my heart wanted to go. Queue the screeching brakes.

The tricky part was that the jobs I was taking on hit on so many of my own personal mission statement desires to create beautiful community, yet it was just not quite right. It was like looking through someone else's glasses, you can still see but everything is a bit fuzzy. When I looked at the business I was creating I realized the prescription was just a little off. It was time to do some digging through my dream bank.

Every idea that I had added to my dream bank had to do with creating community, not through big events but through simply living life together. I was dreaming about dinners set up on beaches and in greenhouses, afternoons bringing women together on flower farms and in kitchens, time around beautiful tables encouraging women to find their own dreams, and of more time to bring our community together for freedom dinners. The problem was, with the current direction of the business there was no space to actually do what my heart was dreaming over. It was time to refocus.

You might be feeling this same pull.

DREAM CATCHER

Are you feeling a check in your own heart?

FOCUS

Is the activity around your dream pushing you closer to your goal or is it pushing you off track?

DREAM CATCHER

What 'you should do' ideas have you been hearing from other people?

Is there any 'worth' to them? Can they help you shape your own ideas in any way?

    The funny thing is that distractions are not always just from external voices. The reminder to stay focused is just as important for our own mental space. As you continue to strengthen your creative muscle it will continue to produce more and more ideas. Internal ideas are hard to shake. They feel attached to us in ways that other people's ideas never can! As your creativity grows, start a dream bank, a 'good idea' list. These lists can be extremely helpful because our hearts dream over what is important to us; your dream bank will show you if you are staying on course.

DREAM CATCHER

What 'I want more time to pour into this' ideas have you been hearing from yourself? Write them down, put them in you can put in your dream bank!

FOCUS

Are you spending time doing activities and projects that are in line with these ideas?

DREAM CATCHER

REFINING

I enjoy the refined — whether it's a gorgeous garden, a coffee shop with the perfect atmosphere, or a meal with delicious flavors. But if you asked, do I enjoy the refining process? Well, I'd probably say no! The problem is that you cannot have the beautiful outcome without the refining.

To refine something is to take it from it's crude beginning and transform it into it's 'finished' product. When we scroll through Pinterest or swipe through Instagram we are seeing the outcome of someone else's refining process. We are seeing their finished product. It's gorgeous but at the same time it is layered with trial and error, practice, tweeking, learning, growing, tears, setbacks, frustrations, wins, hopes, dreams, and critiques. If we could feel the weight of the immense work that each of those images required, we would realize that what *we* are creating is also beautiful; we might just be in a different stage of the refining process.

There are three main stages to the refining process: 1) *separation* is where we sift out the excess, 2) *conversion* is where we turn the idea into action, and 3) *treating* is where we continue to remove the smaller toxins that cloud the final product.

Staying focused and committed to shedding the excess makes space for the refining process. From the outside looking in it can look a bit eclectic. You might be trying new things, new tactics, new classes, new ideas, new ways of parenting, eating and living. But it's through the sifting, the growing, and the changes that your dream will become clearer. This refining gives you the clearest picture of where you are headed. We invite the refining process when we make space to truly look at what we are doing, to ask the hard questions, to listen to our hearts.

When you start chasing your dream, your life, your heart and your mind will tell you more about what is right than anything or anyone. The act of living out your dream refines it. However, yours cannot be the only voice. You need outside eyes and perspectives and, yes, you even need those folks in your life that question your dream.

Come on, fess up! I bet a name or two comes to mind. That person who challenges you. The one that asks such deep *why?* questions that leave you thinking long after your conversation ends, the questions might even make you feel defensive!

Who came to mind?

YOU NEED THESE PEOPLE.

I know!! It's not easy to have your dream questioned, but it is necessary. Think of their questions like a piece of sandpaper. When they ask them, you feel it rubbing you the wrong way.

STOP. Don't say anything. Let them explain.

Now, envision them handing the sandpaper to you. They are handing you a powerful tool. Don't discard it because it feels uncomfortable. Take the question and ask it yourself. Think on it.

What questions have people been asking you?

These questions, and these lovely people who ask them, are an integral part of the refining process. They are giving you the gift of helping you see what is most important to you.

This is not the time to find 'yes men". You need people who are not just your cheerleaders but those that have a clear view of you. You need people who can speak truth in a form that you can hear. You need people who will give time and attention to look critically at your work and give you true and honest feedback. *You need people.*

Outside perspectives can help you refine your dream in ways that you cannot alone. Listen for repeat phrases and ideas. Is everyone saying the same thing to you? If so, listen.

After we had been hosting our freedom dinners for about a year, Aaron and I started throwing around the idea of opening our own coffee house. We wanted to create a space where our community could gather. I dove head-first into researching spaces, coffee sourcing, roasters, equipment, and meeting with business owners. But over and over again throughout this process, friends and family would ask *do you want to have a storefront that is open 365 days a year?*

That question felt like a dream crusher, but, wow! I'm glad people asked. At the same time I was researching our coffee house idea, I was continuing to get requests to create more community events. People's questions, coupled with these requests, forced me to stop and take a good look at what direction I really wanted to go.

It wasn't the questioning that determined my direction, it was my answer to the question. *No, I don't want to be tied down to a storefront during this season of our life.* That answer pointed us to where we are today. Welcome the people who question you. Seek them out. Ask for the sandpaper. Their questions do not determine your direction, your answer does!

**Look back at those questions again*:*

What are your initial feelings?

Does it make you feel defensive or supported? Why?

Does it make you feel like they believe in you? Why?

Does it make you question yourself? Why?

How is it helping YOU define your direction?

_____

If you're reading this and thinking, *I don't have anyone in my life that asks me 'sandpaper' questions,* start looking for them. You might need to invite them in. You may seek them out and ask for advice.

Who do you admire that is a few steps ahead of you?

Who do you admire that is doing something similar to you?

Who do you admire in how they live their life?

Set up meetings with these people. Ask them specifically for help. Ask them how they manage their life, their kids, their work. Ask them for advice on your own life.

I know it's hard to put yourself out there, but it's incredibly powerful! Our connections with people have the ability to sway our emotions, change our direction, adjust what we believe, and help us to decipher what we think. This is why they are necessary. We need outside perspective in order to come to our own conclusions. Be wise in who you invite in, but be open to receive the refining.

HOP TO IT

If you're looking around thinking *What I'm doing now doesn't even look close to what I want to be doing! I'm squeezing out bits and pieces of the thing I like to do and it just feels like less than what I was hoping for.* Don't worry, this is what the beginning looks like.

I'm dreaming of a flower farm and all I've got is one small flower bed.

I'm dreaming of writing books, and all I've got is a few blog posts.

I'm dreaming of running a marathon and all I can do is walk a mile.

I'm dreaming of a photography business and all I can do now is take photos of my kids on my phone.

THAT'S OKAY! The starting line is the furthest point from the finish. It's the beginning and it's okay for the beginning to not look like the end. These first steps should be shakier than the last. We don't start because we have it all figured out, we start in order to figure it out.

So if you're feeling wobbly and shaky, like there is a mountain to climb between where you are and where you want to be, then you are exactly where you should be. You've found the trailhead, now let's keep navigating up the path.

I'm hoping that you're still keeping your people close by. You're going to want cheerleaders along the way. They'll help you stay focused but more so they're going to get you through the nitty gritty work of shaping your dream.

This is the work that will help define it. It might look like sketch books full of art that no one will ever see, meals cooked that no one liked, flowers planted that didn't grow, emails sent that had no response. This is the work of growing roots.

Here's the thing about roots. They are the lifeblood of a plant. Without them the plant will wither and die. But you never see them. The work you do now is the deep work of growing roots. No one will ever know the length and breadth and depth of the deep work you will do. No one will ever know how much time and energy you spend growing your roots. They don't need to.

What they will see are the results. No roots = no growth. The deeper the roots the healthier the plant. The stronger the roots the bigger the tree.

This work you are doing now is vital to the health of your dream. It is essential to the longevity, endurance and impact you will be able to have later as you reach your goals. Yes, it can definitely feel like you are far away from what you envision your end product to be. Having a dream or goal or vision means you are going after something you have yet to achieve. No one says they're dreaming of graduating from college after they've already achieved it! You dream about what could be, which means there is going to be a whole lot of work between where you start and where you end.

HOP TO IT

Did you know that when Starbucks opened their first store in 1971 they did not even sell brewed coffee drinks! All they sold were whole roasted beans. It wasn't until 1986 that they started selling espresso drinks. That means for 15 years Starbucks simply sold roasted coffee. The Starbucks that we know today barely resembles where they started, but what if they had not done the work in those early years? What if they had not figured out how to open a shop, how to roast coffee, how to sell to broader markets?

If I only told you about what Starbucks looked like in the beginning you could easily think that I was talking about any local coffee roaster. Our beginnings can feel a bit normal, like there isn't anything too spectacular. Your beginning might *feel* like it looks like everyone else -- keeping working.

When Nike started, the only place you could purchase their shoes was out of the back of Phil Knight's car, and the shoes weren't even their own design! They were simply purchasing from a Japanese distributor and reselling them. For the first two years of business they sold shoes at track meets as traveling salesmen. It wasn't until they were in business for 7 years that they rebranded as the Nike that we know today, swoosh and all.

Friend, if you are looking around at where you are starting and thinking that it's just small potatoes. You're just a little unknown shop on etsy, or you can barely make it through the first 10 minutes of a long work out, don't give up.
Even when people make comments that make you feel small, like you'll never reach your goal. You might look at your work and feel like they're right. Keep working.

The work in the beginning of growth looks a whole lot different than that of the success we see online and in stories. It should look different. Building the foundation always looks different than adding in the finishing touches. But without the foundation your dream has nowhere to stand.

What does it look like to dive into the deep work of laying a foundation? It looks a whole lot like hard hands-in-the-dirt *work*. Practicing. Growing. Reading. Studying. Asking for advice. Learning. Making mistakes, trying again. Producing what you can. Doing what you can. Taking the opportunities that present themselves and living on the learning curve.

Getting to the big dream is going to take a lot of unseen, unthanked, not pretty, no glam or glitz or recognition kind of work. Don't shy away from it, this is the work that is going to help define the dream. This is the work that is going to get you closer to the end goal. This work is the step to getting to where you want to be.

Whenever you see someone and think *they're so lucky, they had the connections for overnight success.* Think again, do a little digging and find out where they started from. Jimmy Fallon and all of his likable guy-next-door qualities started studying SNL when he was just a kid. All through his childhood he would re-enact SNL skits, practice impersonations, try out for music contests and shows, perform in stage productions and more. He trained most of his life to make it onto SNL and it wasn't until he pursued acting and comedy full time for several years and was turned down from SNL on his first audition that he landed another chance to audition and was invited on to the show. When you see him now and think, *well he grew up in New York, it was probably easier for him to get that job*, think again. There is always a backstory of practice and failure, lessons and hard work that prepared them for what we see today. There is no such thing as overnight success.

Here's the beautiful thing. When you are doing work you love it makes the time in the trenches, the weeks and months and maybe years of building your foundation full of fulfillment. It's the purpose and meaning behind the work that push you on, that keep you focused until you reach those goals. Don't shove aside the time you are investing now as not being valuable since you aren't making a lot of money from it, or getting a million likes on instagram, or getting any community recognition. The value we find in our work comes from how deeply it is connected to our hearts.

What opportunities do you have around you to 'work' on your dream?

Go do that work. Then ask yourself :
What did I like about doing that project, or volunteering for that?

HOP TO IT

Would I want to do it again?

What would I do different next time?

Did it open up more opportunity or ideas?

_____

Repeat this process again and again as you refine your work. As you get closer to your goal - this work is shaping you. It's shaping your dream. It's bringing you closer to where you want to be.

MOMENTUM

Do you remember when you first learned how to ride a bike? You got on and were just figuring out how to get enough forward movement to stay upright. Trying to steer and keep everything going in the right direction felt jerky and awkward, even scary.

This is true for all of us as we start into new things. It feels wobbly and like you're swerving this way and that just trying to keep the thing upright. It takes practice to get things moving forward. Momentum isn't instantaneous, so give yourself a whole lot of grace as you find your balance.

Simply put, momentum is the energy gained by a moving object.

As the object moves, momentum is the force that pushes it faster. The great news is that moving objects hold more energy than those standing still. So even though the beginning stages of your dream might feel like trudging uphill in the mud, you *will* get to the point where momentum takes over. Things will start to feel easier and the gains will be greater.

Let me say this, there WILL be bumps in the road, there WILL be detours, there WILL be seasons where you feel like your dream has gone off course, or been waylaid by life. That's okay. This is what real life looks like; we do not live a perfectly scripted existence. But there are strategies we can take to harness the power of momentum and make sure it's pushing us in the right direction.

When we first started our business, I was wobbling all over the place, starting, stopping, falling, getting back up, brushing myself off and looking around thinking, *What in the world am I doing?* Want to know a little secret? Even though our public business name is Ciderpress Lane, the business name that we report taxes for is Cider House Coffee.

In those beginning days I dove full speed into getting all of the details for our coffee house dream up and running. When we hit the brakes on that concept, it felt like I had fallen off the bike. Here I was with a business name for a coffee house, yet I was spending my time designing weddings and my heart was still at the dinner table whispering away about community and freedom dinners and empowering women. Hello wobbles! Oh my, I can still feel my hesitancy in all of it.

I was looking up and around at other successful event businesses, watching what they were doing, feeling like in order for me to find success my business needed to look like theirs. I welcomed all of the weddings, all of the big events, and as I poured my creative energy into it, the business was getting bigger than I could manage on my own. But my front wheel kept veering off course and pointing me back to the table. As much as I tried, I could not keep the momentum moving forward for a business that was disconnected from my heart. Boy am I glad. That feel of wobbling and swerving and being off balance helped me to see that my bike was heading in the wrong direction, that the momentum of growth was leading me down a different path. So I quietly shut down the wedding side of the business and chose my heart. As a result, this book now exists. As a result, Freedom Dinners are being launched in new communities. As a result, more women and children are now fully supported in safe homes around the world.

Friend, it's okay to feel wobbly when you start out, but it is so very important to pay attention to WHY. Why are you feeling that way?

———————————————

What part about your dream feels like you're riding a bike for the first time?

Do you feel like you are pedaling uphill? What part feels hard?

MOMENTUM

Why do you think it feels hard?

Don't stop now, it's okay to feel off balance! New stuff will do that to you. It is in the consistent repetitive movement forward that we gain our confidence.

Now that you know how to ride a bike, isn't it funny to think back to how hard it was to figure it out! In the scope of life, it didn't take too long to feel like you had found your rhythm. Going after your dream is the same. Once you find your balance, let momentum do what it does best: gain ground exponentially.

One way you can tap into momentum is by finding your gurus. When you begin at anything, you need help to understand what systems will work best for your business, what workouts will fit your schedule, what camera lens to use for specific lighting. There is no need to recreate the wheel. What you are creating will naturally look different from theirs, but take their advice so you can save yourself precious time. The people who are ahead of you can serve as a wealth of wisdom and advice, almost like training wheels. The challenge is when we hear these gurus talk on podcasts and interviews, when we meet them for coffee and ask for their advice, it can feel like a fire hose of information. You might feel like you're drowning in a sea of all the things you need to do now in order to succeed. Every system you need to set up, and every way in which you need to be doing everything better has the potential of crushing you before you ever start.

We may see these people ahead of us and think *if* we work harder and longer we will be able to "catch up". Stop the crazy hustle! Growing a dream takes time. Dreams require momentum. You cannot cram growth into a couple of long days. It's over the weeks, months and years of consistently creating that our dreams take on tangible form. Do what you can now and allow time to multiply your efforts. If you only have 30 minutes a day, do the one thing that is most important to get to the next step: go for a walk to burn a few more calories, listen to one podcast training on how to edit photos, write one blog, clean out one garden bed. And let that be enough. These small steps each day compounded upon each other turn into miles walked, full classes completed, months of blog posts and full and blooming gardens.

We must constantly shake off the rush of trying to catch up to people or businesses that are years ahead of us. Instead use their success as a guide. It's easy to see where they are in their own journey and allow it to deflate us. You are not "behind", you are at a different stage. Your story will look different from theirs but they can act as a compass, not a ruler to be measured against. The goal is not to be them, the goal is to learn from them!

Who do you admire that is a few steps or years ahead of you?

Find out more about them. Where did they start? What lessons have they learned along the way? What would they change about how they reached their goal? Is there a way for them to mentor you? If you can't meet with this person one-on-one then stay connected to their story however you can. Let what you see in them encourage you as you take your own steps forward.

As much as I encourage you to watch folks that are ahead of you, you also need those that are right next to you. They're running the race right now too. Why not run together? It's good to have people who you can lament with, celebrate with, and discuss the things that are frustrating or encouraging right now in this season. Sometimes you need someone to stand like a deer in the headlights with you. We all need to feel that we are not alone.

Who do you have in your life that's running, or walking, or maybe just baby stepping along beside you?

Is it possible to take time to do life together this week or in the near future?

What are the hurdles you're both facing? Jot them down! It's good to be reminded that you are not the only one feeling lost in the busyness of life, lost in the busy calendar, lost in the daily grind!

What do you need in order to jump the hurdle?

Have you hit those hurdles and smacked into discouragement? Are you feeling like the forward movement was put on pause? Maybe the sales have stopped in your etsy store, or the flowers just aren't growing well in your garden, or you're barely gaining in mileage for your upcoming marathon. These plateaus are normal. Here are a few ways to help give momentum a healthy kick in the pants.

What opportunities are you hoping for? (DREAM BIG)

DREAM CATCHER

How can you reach out for the opportunities you are hoping for? (Submit an article to a new blog or magazine, contact a business you admire to see if you can collaborate, go to a new class so you can get a new teacher's perspective, join a new volunteer opportunity)?

MOMENTUM

I know this may seem counterintuitive but sometimes the best way to stay connected to our momentum during the plateau seasons is to help someone who is a few steps behind us. You might be surprised to hear this, but you have valuable encouragement and knowledge to share with them. Lend them a steady hand and allow them to learn from you. You'll be amazed how giving a little of your time to cheer them on will inspire and encourage your heart as well. It will shine light on how far you've come, on all that you have accomplished, on the bits and pieces you have figured out. It will encourage your heart and soul because you will SEE the headway you are making. It will refuel your heart.

You'll leave your conversations inspired to keep at it, encouraged that you are getting closer to your goal and strengthened by the realization that you're doing it!

Who can you encourage that is a few steps behind you?

What has it shown you about where you are at today?

What is it showing you about how far you've come?

One of the greatest benefits of relying on momentum to move us forward is the ability it has to create longevity. If we only rely on our own grit and strength to muscle towards our goal, we will always falter before we reach it. But when we connect to others for encouragement, when we recognize and embrace the fact that the dream will grow and flourish as it's ready, we invite a longevity of spirit that cannot be manufactured by our own strength. Tap into that spirit, the one that connects you to the creator of the universe, that whispers in your heart that you were created for this. Stay connected to that still small voice and keep stepping forward.

GIVE

The more we look up and around us for opportunity to use this beautiful goal, this beautiful life, these beautiful things we're creating, the more we will grow—the more our craft will grow and the more our heart will grow to understand that we are created to live deeply out of the places that bring us the most joy. This is the connection point between the every day and living a life of significance. It is the source of power when we realize *I was created to do this in order to help others.*

For me, this entire adventure started as a way to give back. Hosting the Freedom Dinners opened my eyes to the deep desire in each of us to find ways to use what we love in order to connect us to others.

If you're looking at your craft and thinking, *How the heck can a knitted hat make a difference? Or a handcrafted beverage? Or jewelry, photography, health and fitness, business, accounting, design…?* Whatever your craft, there is a way for you to use it to help others. It will make a difference because it makes ALL the difference to you. It is when we connect the 'dream' to ways to inspiring others, activating others, connecting others that we are truly following our hearts. We are wired to help, it is in the very core of our being. When you get to help in a way that is deeply connected to your heart, it breaths life into you.

But what does this look like?

1. Fundraising

Yes, you can *use* what you do as a way to raise funds to help any organization that your heart is drawn to! There are so many ways to go about this, but basically you're going to volunteer your time in a way that will raise money. You might host an event that raises funds like we do with our Freedom Dinners, or it might be that you will donate your items to the organization to be used to raise funds.

It might be good for you to have a conversation with someone from the organization and ask them what would fit best. They might have an opportunity waiting for someone just like you or ways that they can partner with you. Push aside the fear of asking them how you can help. What you have to offer is valuable.

A few questions to ask if you're going to host your own fundraiser:

- What is the best way for people to donate? (some non-profits host campaign pages directly on their websites to help people like you raise funds!)

- Is there a way for businesses or individuals to give in-kind donations to your event and get a tax credit from the non-profit? If so, how would they like you to organize that end of the donations?

- Are there other individuals in your area that the non-profit can connect you to that are already supporting their work? (bring those like minded folks together!)

- Does the non-profit have any brochures or PR material that they can send your way?
- Would it be okay for you to use their logo on your promo material?

- If you are doing an event with food be sure to contact your local health department so you can follow your county guidelines. There are different rules in every county!

Lastly, the absolute BEST question you can ask is: *What is your biggest need right now?* Then brainstorm how you, doing what you love, can meet that need.

2. Volunteer

Volunteering is the act of giving your time and or resources. Maybe you can use your craft to volunteer for the non profit you want to help. Are you great at marketing? Volunteer to help in that area. Are you great at accounting? Volunteer to help in their accounting department. Do you love arranging flowers? Volunteer to provide flowers for their next event. Are you great at baking? Volunteer to bake for their next fundraiser.

It can also look like you volunteering to use your knowledge to help an individual in need. If you're great at bookkeeping, what about helping a single mom with her finances? If you love cleaning and organizing, what about offering to help your neighbor with her garage sale? If you love cooking, what about making a meal for a family in need?

Volunteering your 'talent' does not mean you have to work at an organization—you can freely give your talent to any individual that is in need of your help.

What you do easily can bless someone else profoundly.

3. Use your craft to create community

Did you know that people like being with you?! I'm serious. You're super cool and when you spend time doing the thing you really love you'll find ALL sorts of other folks that want to be a part of what you're doing. Here's the catch—you have to invite them to join you!

Very few people invite themselves into other people's lives. And for good reason! Kid Rule #5 million: don't invite yourself to someone else's house. So, that means YOU are responsible to open the invitation for people to join you. People might not respond the first time you invite, our hearts are shy. Invite again, invite more people, invite other circles of people, invite folks that you've heard like to do the same thing you do. Open your invitations as wide as your heart will allow. We aren't all big group people and that's okay. Start small and let it grow.

This week, this month, look for opportunities to invite people to join you as you hike, bike, garden, paint, cook, create, grow, work out. Invite people in. You'll be surprised at the community that forms. You'll find the most kindred of spirits in those who are naturally drawn to the things that you are naturally drawn to. And now you have a community of people that are an incredible force for good.

4. Teach Someone Else

Think back to how you got started doing what you love. Who got you started? Who poured time and energy into you to help you get better at it?

Now it's time to give that same gift to someone else. You might be thinking, *I don't have it all figured out, how could I help someone else?* You'll be amazed at how much you know when you start explaining just one aspect of what you do.

Sharing your knowledge helps you see how far you have come. It will encourage your own heart as much as it will equip and inspire someone else's. This sharing of knowledge doesn't have to be in the form of a class. Most of the time it will look like a friend asking you to show them how you plant your garden, a family member asking you to help them with their new camera, a gal you meet at the gym asking you to show her how you plan your workouts, a new mom asking you how you got your kids to sleep at night.

When people ask you for help with a certain area in their life they are shining a spotlight on the area that they see you excelling in. Take it as a compliment and SHARE your knowledge. Even if you feel like you're just tripping along, you are tripping along the path ahead of them. So hold their hand and show them what you've learned.

5. Use it, it's Your Voice!

Your life is your loudest voice. This isn't about the words you speak, this is about what you are choosing to take action on. When your people, your family, your community see you using the thing you love in a way that helps others, they will be inspired to do the same.

None of us wants to be seen as a know-it-all, or like we have it all figured out. But, the truth is, we're all sitting in our own skins feeling the same feelings of figuring-it-out-one-day-at-a-time. Take the heavy load off that you need to be perfect in order to make an impact.

The simple act of using what you're great at to help someone else says it all. Your actions are speaking louder than words ever could.

There are an endless number of ways that we can connect with our communities. Let's share what we have and give of ourselves. I cannot wait to hear about how you are using the life you love as a way to love others.

This is your legacy. These everyday moments, stacked upon each other create the life that you will lead. My prayer is that in the midst of the daily to-dos and must-dos that you have found a deep purpose and meaning. That you have connected with your creator in a way that is continuing to connect your heart to new ways that you can love on the people around you. Make space for this sweet heart of yours. Make space for it to dream and grow, you will never regret it.

DREAM CATCHER

Did you know you are not alone on this journey? There is a mighty tribe of women waiting for *YOU* to come dream with us.

We are doing big things in our every day lives. Pushing back fear, believing in ourselves and realizing that we're all carrying the same desire for significance.

We're changing this world together by doing what we love. We're changing this world by cheering each other. We're changing this world by listening to the small whisperings of our hearts.

It takes courage to step into a new circle of friends, we're here with open arms and a big wide invitation!
We're waiting for you.

www.dreamcatchercommunity.com
Kelly

If you're just not ready to jump in, come hang out with me at @kellywelk